To order additional copies of this book, contact:
Xlibris
844-714-8691
www.Xlibris.com
Orders@Xlibris.com

ISBN: 978-1-6641-9505-9 (sc)
ISBN: 978-1-6641-9506-6 (hc)
ISBN: 978-1-6641-9504-2 (e)

Print information available on the last page

Rev. date: 10/15/2021

IN LOVING MEMORY

AMAYA JEMA YVONNE LASHLEY

APRIL 28, 2001 - OCT 9, 2007

This book is dedicated to the loving memory of my grand-daughter, Amaya Jema Yvonne Lashley, who left us too soon. Her life was a blessing to family and friends. She always brought joy and laughter to anyone who came in contact with her. I hope this book brings joy and laughter to other children.

Jenith Yvonne Lashley

Illustrations by Marvin Tabacon

SAMMY the Pig

2

Petra said, "Sammy

my little pet pig

4

loves to dance and do the jig ."

5

He even laughs and
rolls in the garden
filled with daffodils,

8

which mother and I planted

under the window sill.

Sometimes he lands

upon his head,

And even pretends
that he is dead.

He pushes and roots the daffodils with his snout,

then sneezes and
sneezes until it becomes
a water spout.

It pours and flows
like a river,

20

As he shakes and quivers.

...while playing in the garden filled with daffodils.

Right under my mother's window sill.

Printed in the United States
by Baker & Taylor Publisher Services